TERRIBLE TRACY
A Cautionary Tale

First published in 1989 by Margaret Hamilton Books Pty Ltd
PO Box 28 Hunters Hill NSW 2110 Australia
First published in 1991 in Great Britain
by Collins Educational
London and Glasgow
A Harper Collins company

Book Bus editor Pat Green

ISBN 0 00 313760 0

Produced in Hong Kong by Mandarin Offset

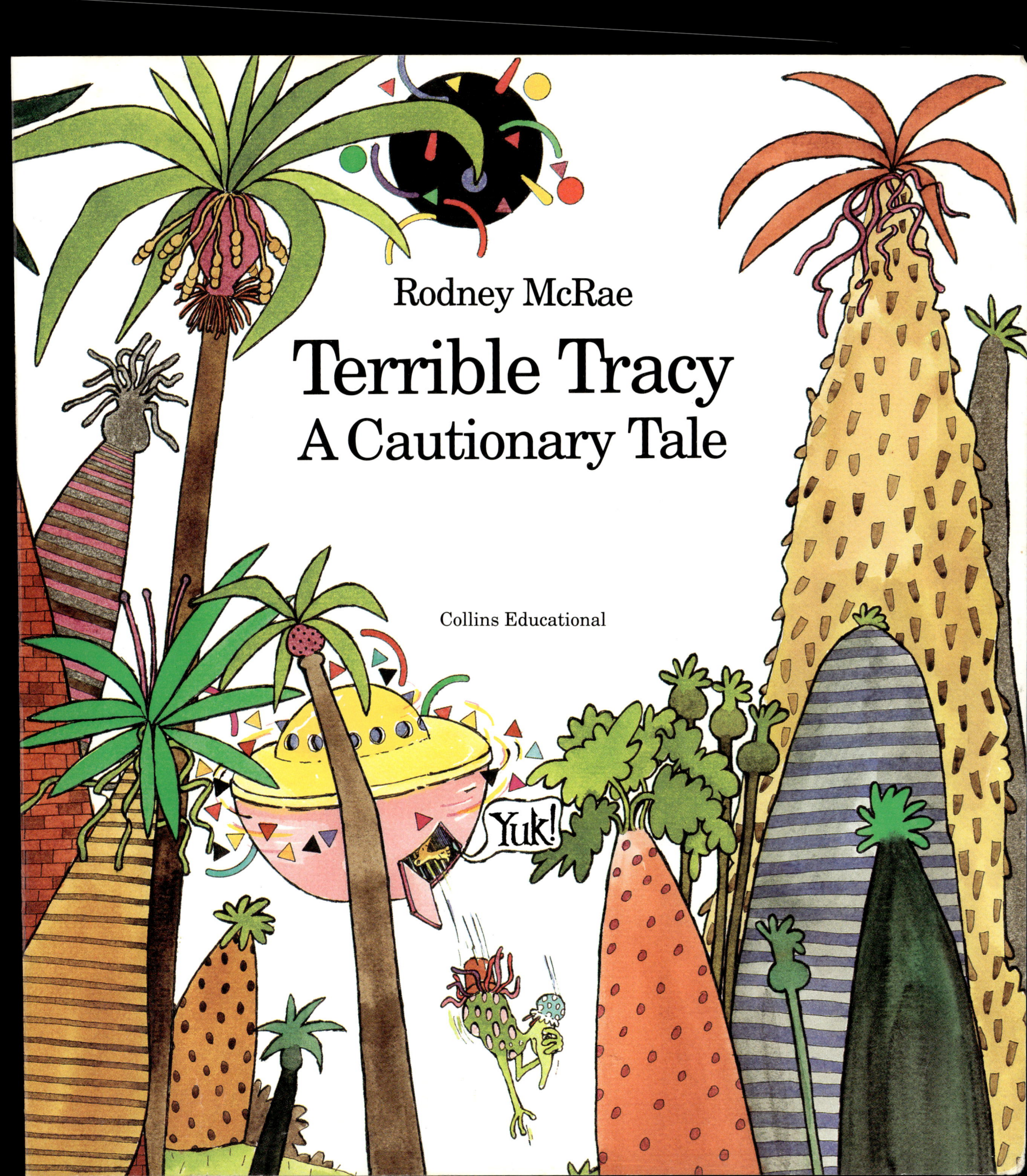

Rodney McRae

Terrible Tracy
A Cautionary Tale

Collins Educational

Yuk!

Tracy was a very mean little girl.

Everywhere she went, she made trouble.

Tracy's parents gave her a very ugly plant for Christmas. Tracy loved it!

She fed the plant on all the food she didn't like herself.

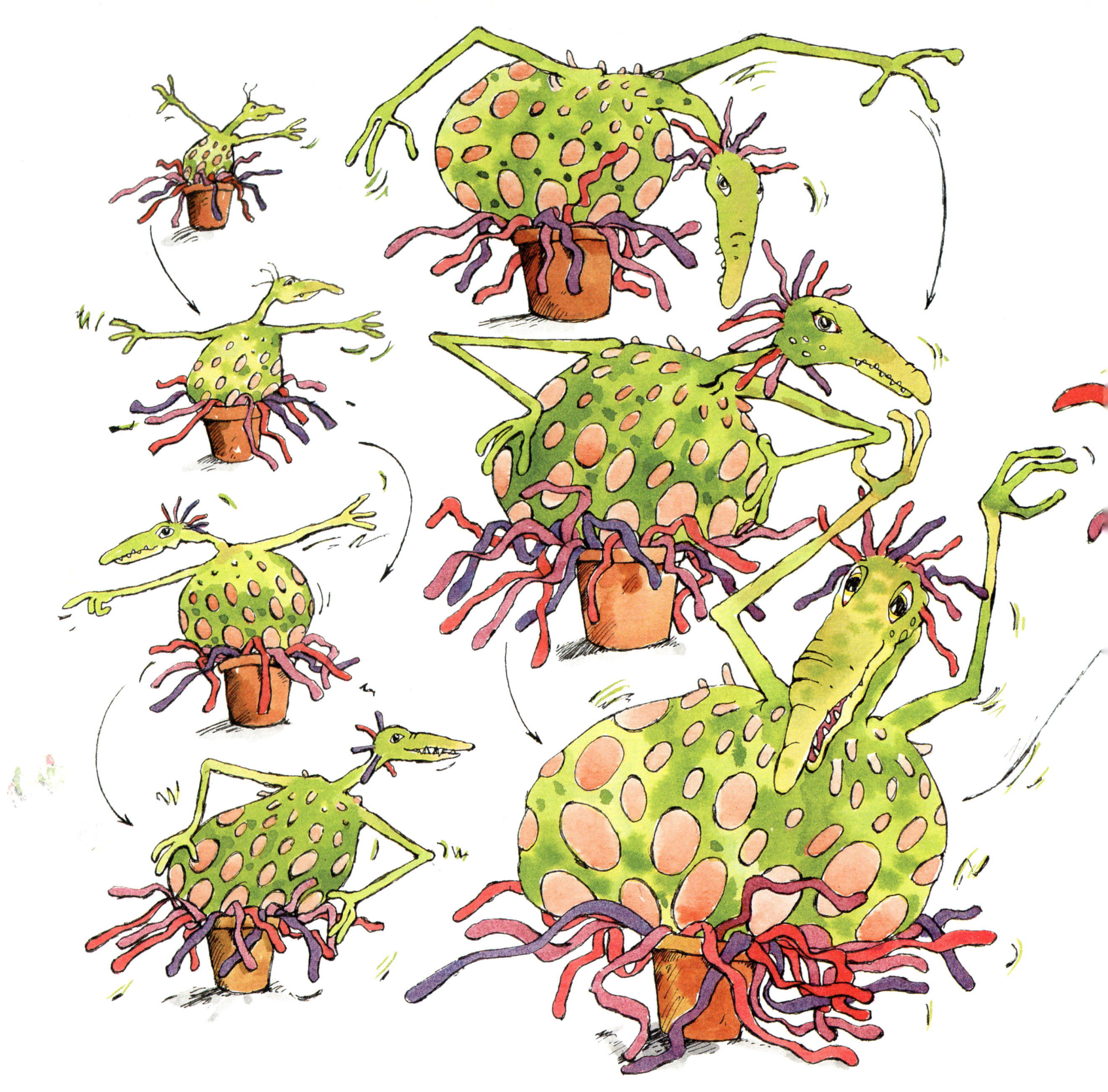

Tracy's plant grew bigger and bigger...

and uglier and uglier.

Every day Tracy took her plant for a walk in the park.

She discovered that it had an insatiable appetite.

One day the plant ate the cat. Tracy's parents
scolded her.

But Tracy's plant took a revenge.

Then Tracy went to school and made trouble...

and the plant helped her.

After school, Tracy made trouble on the bus...

and the plant helped her.

Tracy made trouble in the town...

and the plant helped her.

Very soon the neighbours called the police.

Tracy and her plant were sent away to prison.

Tracy didn't like it there. She made even more trouble...

and the plant helped her.

Very soon the army was called.

Tracy and her plant were banished to a desert island to repent their ways.

"I'm thirsty," said the plant.

"Too bad," said Tracy and she drank all the lemonade,
every last drop.

"I'm hungry," said the plant.

"Too bad," said Tracy and she ate all the
sandwiches, every last crumb.

"You shouldn't have done that," said the plant.